A

SERMON

PREACHED TO THE CONGREGATION

AT THE

Essex Street Church, October 31, 1852,

THE SABBATH AFTER THE INTERMENT OF

HON. DANIEL WEBSTER.

BY NEHEMIAH ADAMS, D.D.
PASTOR OF ESSEX STREET CHURCH, BOSTON.

SECOND EDITION.

BOSTON:
PRESS OF GEO. C. RAND, CORNHILL.
1852.

CORRESPONDENCE.

Boston, November 2, 1852.

Reverend and Dear Sir:—

At a meeting of the Young Men of the Essex Street Congregational Society, held in the Vestry on Monday evening, the first instant, the undersigned were appointed a committee to request of you, for publication, a copy of the discourse delivered by you, on Sabbath morning last, on the decease of the Hon. Daniel Webster.

In performing this pleasant duty, allow us to express individually our earnest desire, that you will be pleased to comply with the urgent request of your young parishioners.

It is our sincere prayer to our Heavenly Father, that you may be spared yet many years to your flock; and we assure you, that we shall at all times delight to assist and cheer you in your labors.

Very truly and respectfully,

THOMAS J. LEE,
MILAN HULBERT,
EDWARD P. DUTTON, } Committee.
FRANCIS F. EMERY,
W. R. BROUGHTON,

To Rev. N. Adams, D.D.

To Messrs. Thomas J. Lee,
Milan Hulbert,
Edward P. Dutton,
Francis F. Emery,
Wm. R. Broughton,
Committee of the Young Men of the Essex Street Society.

My Dear Friends :—

In complying with your renewed request, and with solicitations from other members of our Society, to furnish a copy of my last Sabbath morning's Sermon for the press, I forego my personal preferences, and commit the manuscript to your disposal, for the private use of yourselves and friends.

Very affectionately,
Your Pastor and friend,
N. ADAMS.

Boston, Nov. 6, 1852.

NOTE BY THE COMMITTEE, TO THE SECOND EDITION.

This Sermon was first printed for private distribution among the members of Rev. Dr. Adams' congregation. The edition having been exhausted, and many persons having expressed a desire to obtain the Sermon, the author has kindly permitted this second edition to be published.

December 20, 1852.

SERMON.

I SAMUEL XXV. 1.

AND SAMUEL DIED: AND ALL THE ISRAELITES WERE GATHERED TOGETHER, AND LAMENTED HIM, AND BURIED HIM IN HIS HOUSE AT RAMAH.

THE past week has been to this community a week of unparalleled interest. Since the death of Washington, the decease of no man has produced such an effect upon the hearts of the American people as that which is now the subject of public lamentation. The general grief is unaffected. Words and signs of sorrow do not, and cannot, increase it, but only serve to give it utterance. There is a depth of love in this grief which few men (indeed, a child might write them,) have ever occasioned. There is secret weeping, and sadness of heart, and feelings which can never be expressed.

The origin and early history of this great man; the first steps of his professional career, marked with such success and honors; his statesmanship; his great national services; his power as an orator; the unsurpassed excellence of his writings; his influence as a public teacher; the wonderful combination, in his thoughts, of the explanatory and illustrative with the sublime and elevating, gratifying the common apprehension with the consciousness of understanding him, and yet making us respect him in his unattainable power of statement and argument; his failure to receive the nominal reward of our republican gratitude; his death, succeeding rapidly the recent and final decision that he never should be the Chief Magistrate of the nation; and the sublime and touching incidents of his last hours, combine to make this man the subject of an interest which falls short of idolatry by a less degree than that awakened by the decease of any excepting Moses, and Samuel, and the few, since their day, in the history of the old nations, and the very few of this young republic.

Were the language of mere eulogy required or expected, the pulpit would not be the place, nor the Sabbath the time, nor ministers of the Gospel the men for such service. This great man is above all praise in all that made him truly great. There are some, but they are few, that can approach to describe or measure that greatness, who do not, thereby, place themselves in the position of men at the bottom of pictured pyramids or giant trees.

But reflections which the most common mind will suggest in connection with a great event, such as words cannot adequately express, not unfrequently convey instruction, and satisfy the wish that labors to feel and speak upon the subject justly. By this thought, I am encouraged to contribute a humble offering, not to the memory of our distinguished friend, but, as becomes me better, to your reflections, in making a profitable use of our bereavement.

I. We have lost a great public benefactor.

One of the distinguished blessings which the God of nations bestows upon a people in the persons of great and useful men, is taken away.

A truly great lawyer at the bar is an eminent blessing. The rights of persons and property find in him one of those great safeguards which free governments provide for us, — not in the arbitrary judgment, right or wrong, of a Sovereign, nor of the Judiciary, but in reason, employed to elicit truth and commend the cause on trial to the enlightened judgment of the community, whose sober, settled opinion is of the first importance in free states. A truly great and just lawyer, rising above artifice, and resting his cause on truth, is one whom the people of such countries as ours should honor and cherish as among the best defences of those private interests which make up the sum of public safety and happiness. Our departed friend was such a man. Whether defending chartered rights in behalf of a literary corporation; or helping one of our towns to convict and punish the assassin; or merchants to recover the insurance on their property; or the underwriters to defend themselves against fraud, he has rendered invaluable services to his generation.

He has finished his professional career, and his brethren, in doing homage to his talents and worth as a member of the bar, while they deepen our sorrow at the loss of him, comfort us, by the assurance which we have in them, that his example and influence not only survive, but will not be wholly without compeers.

Our nation has not lost a greater benefactor since the death of its founders. He has preserved us, under God, from foreign wars; and when we say this, we say more than imagination can represent. There have been times during his various administration of affairs in which we have all felt as when we stand upon the deck of a powerful ship, with our eye upon the man at the wheel, and see how, by a skilful motion, he makes the ship pass more easily over a swelling billow, and go with safety over sunken rocks, where the dimpling waters reveal, to the experienced eye, the extremest peril.

This man has done as much, by his various influence, for this union of great States, as any other since that "Farewell Address" was written, which he had so faithfully learned, and which he has taught us to consider. We look upon him, in this respect, as an instrument in the hands of God, who has not ceased, and, we trust, will not cease, to use him for this great purpose, to keep us as a nation from dismemberment. You will do me the justice to believe that I do not speak from party feeling, as I never have done here, when I express the belief that posterity, and not a very distant generation, will adjudge him to have been disinterested and patriotic in his compromise measures with relation to Slavery in the United States. Posterity will not look at those acts of his, as we do, in near connection with an elevation to the Chief Magistracy, but will have the advantage of distance in looking at other acts of his life to interpret his feelings and motives here. A man who spoke as he did to South Carolina and the South in his second speech in the Senate of the United States on

Mr. Foot's resolutions, could not afterward have cringed to chaffer with her for her votes, falsifying the whole spirit and many of the principles of that speech, without doing a greater degree of violence, I will not say to his nature, but, to human nature, than impartial judges will hereafter believe to have been possible. Nor will posterity, I venture to assert, suffer him long to lie under the imputation of seeking to aid and abet the system of slavery by any thing which he did in connection with the Fugitive Slave Law, whatever effect that law may have to perpetuate slavery. I do not seek to express an opinion here with regard to the exciting and controverted topics of the day, but to utter the strong convictions of my own mind with regard to the uprightness of this lamented public servant, in his connection with them.

Were I speaking, as I think I am not, to any who are politically his enemies on account of his influence in the re-enactment of a former statute relating to domestic slavery, I would pray them, by the conciliating influences of his death, to consider this: Whether Mr. Webster, in dealing with this great moral and political evil, may not have regarded himself in some such position as that of Franklin when he provided the lightning conductors. The comparison does not admit of an extended application, and I do not wish to extend it, but merely to suggest, that Mr. Webster's avowed principles and political services warrant the belief that, seeing the North and the South marshaling their angry forces in the heavens over our heads, he sought to apply a means of protection and safety to the whole land, to save the country from events by which not only freemen, but slaves themselves, would be involved in calamities more direful, in his view, even than slavery. In these measures, I must express my persuasion, he acted from a disinterested love to his whole country, and did that which he considered essential to the highest good, whatever the result may be. I would not exaggerate his influence in keeping us from disunion, but, the sun that went down on the day of his funeral left this nation, still, the United States of America, and did not veil himself from the sight of "broken and dishonored fragments of a once glorious union; States dissevered, discordant, belligerent; a land rent with civil feuds and drenched in fraternal blood." * When our advocate for union uttered these words in the Senate of the United States, he did not know that God would make him, as we believe He has done, one of the principal instruments to fulfil, thus far, his own great wish, to answer his mighty prayer. May the benign influence of supreme love to God in Christ soon enable us to approach every subject of national difficulty with the spirit of peace and good will. And now, as we sail away together in our national bark from the sea-girt tomb of our pilot, O that we might all agree, North, South, East, and West, to throw into the waves, as a sacrifice, our unkind feelings, our bitter words, on the subject of American Slavery. Let the land have a Sabbath with regard to this subject, and let that Sabbath be the long, long days of our mourning for this great patriot, our country's friend.†

* Second Speech on Mr. Foot's Resolution, at the close.

† In confirmation of the conviction expressed in the foregoing paragraph, I will state the following anecdote: A clergyman, well known to my hearers,

II. We cannot but notice the hand of God in appointing this death just at the eve of the Presidential election.

After all, it is of very little consequence, in one point of view, who fill the thrones and seats of power in this world. The blessed and only Potentate has designs with regard to this nation, which we and the men of our choice will fulfil, in perfect ignorance, however, at the time, of the use which is made of us. The result of this next Presidential election will be hailed as the triumph of a party; but they who look upon it from the world of light, where every thing is judged of in connection with God's great plan in human affairs, will see in it a step toward some important purpose in the mind of God, with whom the tumult of the people, in their elections and political victories, is like the measured tramp of a host obeying the word of command in a well appointed evolution. The past forbids any thing but hope and confidence in God with regard to our coming history; but we are in the hands of One to whom a nation is an individual thing, to be preserved or broken, prospered or afflicted, in his merciful providence or righteous judgment. Foreign wars may await us; entanglement with the concerns of other nations, either to our own hurt, if not perdition, or, to spread

says, that having occasion not long since to meet Mr. Webster on some official business, the conversation turned upon the compromise measures, and Mr. Webster's connection with them. Mr. Webster said, "It seemed to me at the time, that the country demanded the sacrifice of a human victim, and I saw no reason why the victim should not be myself." The clergyman says that Mr. W.'s manner evinced such sincerity and deep patriotic disinterestedness, that he was moved to tears, which do not cease to start at every recollection of the interview.

the principles of political freedom, and thus advance the kingdom of Christ. Measures may be taken to give the Roman Catholic influence a greater predominance here, or to fortify our institutions against it. Industry and the useful arts, inventions and discoveries, may be greatly stimulated or palsied; good morals and religion may receive countenance; the righteous may flourish in the abundance of peace, or the wicked may walk on every side. There is no such thing as pause or rest in our destiny for years to come. For good or ill, we shall move round the orbit where the great Builder's hand has launched us, either avoiding, by the help of that same hand, those bodies which cross our track, or receiving damage. Whatever happens to us, our rulers, our parties, our individual votes will have produced it, instrumentally; and will fulfil the decrees of the great God. We cannot doubt that the removal of our distinguished fellow citizen, just at this time, will have an important influence, but we know not how, upon the event of the coming election. He who knows times and seasons, (and the number of our months are with Him,) has ordered this decease in such a manner that its powerful effect is felt in season to influence the feelings, and the opinions, and the votes of so many, as will, perhaps, decide our political destiny for another presidential term. We cannot fail to notice and to feel the power of this coincidence. This great man dies and goes to his long home. A Sabbath ensues, and the nation in her temples is weeping and praying over this great decease. The week days resume their round, and twenty-three millions of people choose their rulers, and change their national administration.

It is done in a day, but the end is with God. The hand of God is in this thing, preparing the way for such a result as He shall choose. It was through the agency of another Daniel, in former days, that a heathen king was compelled to utter these words, which may instruct us, and appropriately dwell upon our hearts and upon our lips: — "And at the end of the days, I, Nebuchadnezzar, lifted up mine eyes unto heaven, and mine understanding returned unto me, and I blessed the Most High, and I praised and honored him that liveth forever, whose dominion is an everlasting dominion, and his kingdom is from generation to generation; and all the inhabitants of the earth are reputed as nothing; and he doeth according to his will in the army of heaven, and among the inhabitants of the earth; and none can stay his hand, or say unto him, What doest thou?"

Suppose that Mr. Webster had received the nomination for the presidency by the late Baltimore Convention, as many of us desired and expected. What a day the coming second of November would have been to one of the great political parties throughout the land. What would they have done? What could they have done? Distracted with disappointment and sorrow, with no time for concerted action, their hearts would have melted, their knees would have smitten together, their faces would have gathered blackness. I speak to you who are members of that party, not as a politician, but as a believer in God's providence, and ask you to see the hand of God in your affairs. Could the Almighty have spoken to you with an audible voice at Baltimore, disclosing his purposes, He might have said to you respecting this candidate: "Seeing his days are determined, the number of his months are with me, I have appointed his bounds that he cannot pass, turn from him that he may rest, till he shall accomplish as an hireling his day." When you or your representatives were at Baltimore, God was there, and there were many devices in men's hearts; "but the counsel of the Lord, that shall stand."

The great fault of our age is, Low views of God. The Almighty has now reached down his hand; He is almost as impressively present with us as he was when he stood on the top of Nebo, and called Moses thither to die, and Israel saw the form of their leader disappear into that presence which no man can see and live. Is this great departure, one week preceding an election, an accident? "Verily there is a God that ruleth in the earth!" "Not a sparrow falleth to the ground without Him." This great man, in the time and manner of his fall, was, in the purposes of God, of more value than many sparrows. May the fear of this ever present God fall on you, and his excellency make you afraid.

III. The last days and hours of this distinguished man are eminently instructive.

Jesus Christ and his religion disdain no man's love and advocacy, while they are beholden to no man for his acceptance of them. We should not rest our confidence in the Bible upon the opinions and feelings of men; still, we are confirmed in our faith when wise and great men are of our opinion. Irreligion, sceptical opinions with regard to the Scriptures, transcendental views of Christ and the

Apostles, are rebuked by the testimony of this pre-eminent human intellect. Modern unbelief had, in its own conceit, fixed a great stone at the door where it had buried our Saviour and his religion. God has raised up a man of your own city and people, whose countenance is, to you, like lightning, and he has rolled away that stone and sat upon it. As defenders of the credibility of the christian faith, we feel that henceforth our labors with some of our fellow men are greatly lessened. Spiritual religion cannot, indeed, be attested by any who are not themselves spiritually enlightened by the Holy Spirit; but the evidences of christianity can be appreciated by the human understanding, and have been maintained by the wisest and greatest of men in every age, whom, however, unbelievers regard only as professional writers, and employed advocates of religion. Now, God has raised up among us one to whose calling and to whose death-bed it did not belong, professionally, to assert the truth of the christian religion. He died in the firm belief that the Holy Scriptures are the word of God, and that there is salvation only through Jesus Christ.

It is creditable to the state of the public conscience on the subject of religion, that, during the two or three days when it was known that Mr. Webster must die, the great concern seemed to be, to know something with respect to his religious preparation for death. Every thing which was reported on this point was read and remarked upon with no common interest. All wished and prayed that this beloved man might die the death of the righteous, and his last end be like his. And there is a general gratification in the community at the serious feelings and religious expressions which gave character to his last hours. It is, then, an established truth among us, never more fully received or durably impressed upon the minds of all than now, that religion alone can prepare a man to meet his God and his judge. In many companies of a confidential nature, you have no doubt heard the question considered with the deepest kindness and tenderness, May we not hope that Mr. Webster is a true Christian? His peculiar exposures to temptation, on the dangerous summit which he occupied before the country, and in the scenes of exciting interest through which, as a statesman and a politician, he was called to pass, and from the unmeasured admiration with which he was surrounded, must have required more than unaided mortal strength to pass through them without delinquency. How far he succeeded, or whether any of us, in his circumstances, would have needed more charity in the judgment of others concerning us, than he, it is not useful or suitable to inquire. Is there any thing in his writings, from first to last, that betrays a corrupt mind, a vicious imagination, or a disposition to trifle with serious things?

He was in the habit of praying with his family, in doing which, surely no worldly motive could play its part. Great interest has been expressed to know how he spent the hours of the Sabbath, as indicating whether he had that spiritual mind which loves the day, because it loves the God who made it, and the things which it is set to promote. We all know, without being told, that, like us, he was a sinner before God, and could not be saved for being a great man, or an eloquent man, or a useful man; but, like Paul, must have been "found in Christ, not having his own righteousness, but the righteousness which is of God through faith." The same essential truths were as appropriate at his dying bed as they will be at yours; it was needful for him, as for you, to repent and believe in Christ, "in whom we have redemption through his blood, even the forgiveness of sins;" and when his spirit stood before his God, he left behind him, as he left his mortal part, every thing which could constitute a claim upon the divine favor, and only for his heartfelt trust in the Saviour of the world, could he, with the rest of the sinful race, be justified and saved. The throng of great and just men made perfect who were moved at his coming, looked at him, not as some of them saw him on Plymouth Rock, and Bunker Hill, in the Senate chamber, and in the Court room, but, as a fallen son of Adam, who, by his sins, had, like other men, lost heaven; and the question there, and the only question, was, Has he accepted Jesus Christ as He was offered to him in the Gospel? The gate was no more strait, nor the way more narrow, for him, to enter into life, nor was it a jot or tittle easier, or in any respect otherwise, than it is for you. For there is salvation in Christ for all, and not "in any other; for there is none other name under heaven given among men whereby we must be saved."

He loved the christian religion. He loved and cherished the christian ministry; and the clergy throughout the christian world are indebted to him for his feelings and expressions with regard to them. They, in their turn, have loved and revered him in a measure not exceeded by their feelings toward any cotemporary.

We all know that death enshrines every one who, by any exercise of hope, we can believe is saved; that great faults, and even known sins and bad habits, are regarded as atoned for by dying; the piteous looks and tones on the death bed being inconsistent, in our minds, with any thing but compassion and mercy. There is always much false theology lurking in affectionate or complaisant sentiments at such a time as this, and we must be careful not to contradict established truths, and our avowal of them, when we are under the influence of popular enthusiasm. If we declare our belief that a soul is saved, justice and kindness to ourselves and others demand that we rest our belief on scriptural reasons. We must not be deceived, nor deceive others, with regard to the conditions of pardon and salvation. There is not one Gospel for the living, and another for the dying. The warnings and threatenings, the promises and consolations, which you read in the Bible and hear from the pulpit in your health and strength, are as true, they are the same, when you are dying, as ever. We say of our beloved friend that which you will say of each other, and of each of us, ministers of the Gospel: If he repented of his sins, and believed on the Saviour of the world, we, if we do the same, shall meet him in heaven. If you feel sure that he is safe, prepare to die with christian faith and hope; if you still inquire for more information, containing evidence to satisfy you that he died a regenerated man, see that you yourself experience and do those things which you deem satisfactory evidence of acceptance with God.

What a subject death found, when it approached him. How hard a task to conquer his life. Such a vitalized death, we seldom knew. He speaks, in the very act of dissolution, and says, "I still live." Could the king of terrors have relented and trailed again his dart, this was the man for him to spare. Inexorable sentence! "passed upon all men, for that all have sinned." Who can claim or expect exemption now? Our Presidents, our Senators, our Counsellors, our Judges, our Ministers of the Gospel, the chief Captains, and the Kings of the earth, who slew all these? If sin destroys the body, if it defiles every thing honorable and beautiful in the outward man by death, what must its ravages be in the soul, which is its proper seat!

And now he has "lain still, and is quiet, and sleeps, and is at rest, with kings and counsellors of the earth, which built desolate places for themselves." Who will be the President of the United States for the next four years, is a question whose interest with him has been absorbed, and, for the time, forgotten, in a question personal to himself, which has now been settled for eternity. He once made a public profession of his faith in Christ, before a christian Church in a New England village. That day and that transaction now seem more important to him, than this bawble, — the Presidential chair. Could he return, I cannot resist the conviction, he would think more of the Church of Christ, of its devotional privileges and opportunities, and the spread of the Gospel of Christ in the earth; as no doubt all in heaven would, could they enjoy the privilege, which we still have, of living and of serving Christ in a world like this.

One thing even he might find it hard to do; and that is, to improve the moral tone, and the intellectual power and beauty, of his writings. He has left the world a rich legacy in his works, and if some one will add to them a volume of the eloquent and impressive words which his death has occasioned, and shall occasion, at the bar and in the assemblies of the nation, the measure of his ability to instruct the world will be full.

His death makes us all love one another. It makes it easy for these hard, cold hearts of ours, which the world rifles of their affections, it makes it easy for them to show feeling and not be ashamed. We love those who, by their touching emblems of sorrow in their windows and places of business, have helped our weeping. Our country, if our sins do not prevent, will be more one country than before; our Presidents will strive to rule over the whole nation, and not serve a party; our public men will remember that they must die, and live more like dying men. They called him, in the language of the great poet of nature, "the foremost man of all the world." He was the rearmost of an age in our history, which nothing but hope and cheerful trust in God prevents us from calling our golden age. The men who have conducted the country hitherto on her high career, are now all gone. Young men in professional life, see before you the path to honorable distinction and usefulness, and to the inevitable gratitude of a great nation, at least at your decease, and to the attainment of a name which is more precious than rubies. Remember the testimony which this man has given you, that "the fear of the Lord is the beginning of wisdom."

In the borrowed language of this great orator, in Fanueil Hall, just after the receipt of some disastrous tidings in an election, we say, as we now return from burying him in his house in Ramah, "All is not lost." Even he is not lost to us. His influence is ten-fold greater than ever. Who made this man, and gave him to this nation? Who is the Prince of the kings of the earth? HE lays his right hand upon our nation, and says, "Fear not, I am the first and the last; I am he that liveth and was dead, and behold I am alive for evermore, and have the keys of hell and of death." This past week, in reading the works of this great man, and the beautiful and touching anecdotes of his early life, and the skilful and pathetic portraitures of his character, and seeing the tokens of the deepest universal sorrow which our land has felt for, at least, one generation, and in thinking of him now, in the house appointed for all living, I have felt the need of some man, some fellow man, whom I can love and not lose, as we have lost him. I "have found Him of whom Moses in the law, and the prophets, did write, Jesus of Nazareth," "the same yesterday, to-day, and forever." "And his name shall be called," — and never more appropriately than now, — "Wonderful, Counsellor, the Mighty God, the everlasting Father, the Prince of Peace." All that was great, beautiful, good, in this departed friend, was derived from Jesus Christ, by whom all things were created, whether they be thrones, or dominions, or principalities, or powers. He Himself "is fairer than the children of men."

In the declining sunlight of an October day, not long since, I saw the trees of the wood, beautiful in the melancholy change of their leaves, which a rising wind was showering to the ground. The rays of the sun fell upon a tall pine of fresh and brilliant green; and wondering at it for a moment, as out of season, I was reminded that the evergreens put forth fresh spires in autumn, when the leaves of other trees fall. As the evergreen never seems so beautiful and striking as when the other trees are stripped of their foliage, so when friends, and great and useful men, die, there is One, born for adversity, who makes even decay and desolation cheerful, in being, himself, the pledge of immortality, the Resurrection and the Life.

Fellow citizens, fellow sinners, fellow travellers to eternity, love "Immanuel, God with us," your Saviour and friend, with the love and zeal with which you regard your great earthly brother and friend, and your interests for eternity are safe. Open the New Testament, read any chapter in the life of Christ, and you will find far more to love and praise, than in all the words and deeds of men. When our fellow countrymen shall love and worship Christ, according to the injunctions of the second Psalm, and, in consequence, shall be consistent members of christian Churches, in such numbers as to create a public religious sentiment, then the country will be safe. Then we can discuss and settle political and moral questions without danger or serious difficulty. Supreme love to Jesus Christ is not a mere frame of mind for private devotion, an experience pertinent only to the secret life of a believer; it must pervade the public mind, it must influence the spirit and principles of the rulers and of the citizens. Let no one say, 'This is too much to expect.' For is not this the religion foretold by Prophets as destined to be universal? At the name of

Jesus is not every knee to bow, and every tongue to confess him to be Lord? Jesus Christ, upon whose head are many crowns, and at whose feet our Webster now sees that there is no crown, in earth or in heaven, that should not be laid, claims your supreme love. While you appreciate the excellence, and almost worship the memory, of one, who, after all, is only a nobler worm than you, remember that there is One who made you, and died for you, and will be your final Judge, who says, "He that loveth father or mother more than me, is not worthy of me, and he that loveth son or daughter more than me, is not worthy of me." This claim is either presumption, or, it implies infinite obligations on our part. This week has proved that men can love intensely. It has, in the same connection, witnessed an enforcement of those words; "Cease ye from man whose breath is in his nostrils, for wherewith is he to be accounted of?" The Saviour of the world claims your highest and best affections. We will not be ashamed of Him, nor of his words, in the midst of this generation. We shall one day see Him coming in his glory, and all his holy angels with Him; the small and great will be at his bar; He will "separate them one from another;" his awards will have reference to their feelings and conduct toward Him. Remember, then, his commandment, and his gracious words: "IF ANY MAN SERVE ME, LET HIM FOLLOW ME; AND WHERE I AM, THERE SHALL ALSO MY SERVANT BE; IF ANY MAN SERVE ME, HIM SHALL MY FATHER HONOR."

www.ingramcontent.com/pod-product-compliance
Lightning Source LLC
LaVergne TN
LVHW011146110826
845150LV00008B/2534

* 9 7 8 1 4 1 8 1 9 1 7 7 1 *